I0802130

IMAGES
of America

THE ATHENAEUM

On the Cover: The *Turner* (gymnastics) movement was a formidable one and was a vital part of the Athenaeum. Here, both women and men participate in an indoor baseball game at the gymnasium at Das Deutsche Haus. (Courtesy of Indiana Historical Society.)

IMAGES
of America

THE ATHENAEUM

Rick Hofstetter and Jane Simon Ammeson
Introduction by Marsh Davis

ARCADIA
PUBLISHING

ISBN 978-1-4671-0460-9

Published by Arcadia Publishing
Charleston, South Carolina

Printed in the United States of America

Library of Congress Control Number: 2019950416

For all general information, please contact Arcadia Publishing:
Telephone 843-853-2070
Fax 843-853-0044
E-mail sales@arcadiapublishing.com
For customer service and orders:
Toll-Free 1-888-313-2665

Visit us on the Internet at www.arcadiapublishing.com

Author Rick Hofstetter is pictured at the Story Inn, another historic landmark he saved. (Jane Simon Ammeson.)

Contents

Acknowledgments

The Athenaeum stands today because of the courage, vision, and tenacity of the people who built it and later saved it. This is the first book to specifically pay homage to that building and to the Teutonic culture that left its indelible print upon it. I sincerely hope that it is not the last.

Over the years, Jane Ammeson has suffered through my enthusiastic ramblings about the Athenaeum, and it was her idea to approach Arcadia with the intention of publishing a book about it. It never would have occurred to me that this epic story would be of interest to a wide audience. Credit Jane with having that vision.

More than a quarter-century ago, J. Reid Williamson Jr., president of Historic Landmarks Foundation of Indiana Inc., decided that the Athenaeum should be preserved at all costs. His measures to save it appear, in retrospect, bold and innovative. Reid has passed on, mission accomplished, and his organization continues to save other architectural treasures in Indiana, today under the name of Indiana Landmarks. We dedicate this book to Reid, because without his efforts and Indiana Landmarks' considerable clout, the Athenaeum would not be standing today, and there certainly would not be this book to talk about it.

Marsh Davis has filled the shoes of that great man, and we owe Marsh as well as Indiana Landmarks for throwing heft behind this book. Among its many good deeds, we can credit Indiana Landmarks for being an invaluable source of photographs and newspaper accounts. Suzanne Rollins Stannis, director of heritage education and information, has the wisdom of Solomon and the patience of Job. Also, big thanks to Paige Wassel, editorial manager of marketing and communication.

Thanks also to architect Ronald Flick, who besides being a gifted architect is an avid historian and is active in many German-American organizations. He currently serves as the head of the Indiana German Heritage Society. His book *Jasper & Huntingburg* is about Dubois County, Indiana, which also boasts strong Germanic roots. Ron's family came over in 1848 along with many other Freethinkers who settled in Indiana at that time. Ron supplied many of the wonderful photographs in this book. Thank you!

We also express our sincerest gratitude to the Indiana Historical Society (IHS), which holds and preserves the treasures of Indiana's past and granted us easy and unfettered access to materials that proved crucial to completing this book. Kudos especially to Nadia Kousari, visual reference librarian at the IHS, Susan Sulton, director and digital assistant, and Amy Vedra, director of reference, who accepted our frantic pleas for help as this book's deadline loomed. IHS provides considerable support for Indiana authors and must implicitly know that every author is a procrastinator. Another big thank-you to Bill Selm, 2019 Hoosier American of the year. Bill researched and wrote the National Historic Landmarks nomination for the Athenaeum.

In researching this book, we probed the minds, memories, and files of Giles Hoyt, Sawyer Rank, Ruth Reichmann, and Frank and Judy Mueller. Each of them played significant roles in the Athenaeum's revival. Though officially retired from Indiana University, Giles and Ruth remain active in efforts to preserve German culture and its relevance to the Athenaeum. They were responsible, together with Ruth's late husband, Eberhard, in bringing the Max Kade German-American Center into the Athenaeum. The center now serves as a link to the building's German past for its increasingly diverse visitors.

—Rick Hofstetter

The manuscript for this book was nearly completed when Rick Hofstetter tragically died. I have tried to carry on, now seeing this book as a memorial to his work in and love of historic preservation. For all those visiting the Athenaeum, please raise a glass of good German beer in his honor.

—Jane Simon Ammeson

Introduction

Das Deutsche Haus; the Athenaeum; the "A"—call it what you will, this building has survived decades of political and social change, physical neglect and disinvestment, changing tastes in architecture, and the wear and tear of intensive use. In the face of all of that, the Athenaeum stands today as one of Indiana's happiest preservation successes, a resilient and beloved landmark that brims with life.

Designed by architects Bernard Vonnegut and Arthur Bohn in the German Renaissance style and built from 1893 to 1898, its significance to our nation's German American heritage was recognized in 2016 when it was declared a national historic landmark by the US Department of the Interior. Historically, it served as a center of culture and commerce. Music, education, athletics, philanthropy, and, of course, food and drink, abounded. That tradition survives at the Athenaeum with extraordinary energy and continuity, and while the German American connection is embedded in the Athenaeum, the building now serves the broad spectrum of our community.

Like many historic properties, the Athenaeum faced a grim fate just a few decades ago. Thanks to the creation of the Athenaeum Foundation in 1991, led by Rick Hofstetter, the building's long slide into decay was arrested. The new foundation set about the task of raising millions of dollars and engaging Indianapolis's cultural and philanthropic community. It worked. Today, the Athenaeum is more vibrant that at any time in its history. Few buildings anywhere can boast of such diverse use and relevance to new generations.

As work on this book was drawing to a close, we learned of the heartbreaking, untimely death of the Athenaeum's greatest champion, Rick Hofstetter. It is only fitting that this book be dedicated to Rick, a remarkable man whose legacy will live on in the Athenaeum, the irreplaceable landmark that stands and thrives today because of Rick's vision and leadership.

—Marsh Davis
President, Indiana Landmarks

One

Coming to America

German immigration to "Amerika" began even before there was a Germany, with many immigrating to the United States following the failure of an 1848 revolution designed to introduce democratic reforms into the governments of the German states. They were often called "Forty-Eighters." The political unification of Germany occurred very late—on January 18, 1871, to be precise—but by then, Germans had already fought in the Revolutionary War, and millions of them already called America *Heimat* (homeland). America offered a chance to start anew. According to the 1870 census, 78,060 German-born residents lived in Indiana; the state's total population at that time was 1,682,638. The desire to form cultural enclaves meant that German immigration to America was distributed unevenly. German immigrants attracted even more German immigrants. A large number settled in America's upper Midwest, creating a "German Belt" stretching from Pennsylvania well into the Rockies. Today, the great cities of Indianapolis, Cincinnati, Milwaukee, Minneapolis–St. Paul, St. Louis, Des Moines, and others are overwhelmingly populated by those of German ethnicity. (Courtesy of Ronald Flick.)

Das Deutsche Haus, later known as the Athenaeum, was founded by the Socialier Turnverein Aktiengesellschaft, or "Stock Association" (*turnen* means "to practice gymnastics," and *Verein* translates to "club" or "union"). This organization financed the Athenaeum's construction by issuing shares of stock to members of the city's prosperous and fast-growing German community. Among these immigrants were members of the Turners, an athletic and political organization founded in Germany during the second decade of the 19th century. Turners quickly established societies (known as *Turnverein* or *Turngemeinde*) in the American cities in which they settled. These societies served as athletic, political, and social centers for German communities in the United States. Clemens Vonnegut was a co-founder of the Socialier Turnverein in Indianapolis in 1851. (Courtesy of Bass Photo Co. Collection, IHS.)

For all new arrivals, no matter their nationalities or ethnicities, preserving their heritage while becoming part of their adopted country was of utmost importance. Every city with a significant German immigrant population had German-language newspapers until America's entry into World War I in 1917. Indeed, in 1900, German newspapers accounted for most of the non-English newspapers published in the United States. At one point, Indianapolis had dozens of them, including the *Freie Presse von Indiana* (in print from 1853 to 1866), the *Indiana Deutsche Zeitung* (1874–1877), the *Indiana Volksblatt* (1848–1875), and the *Täglicher Telegraph* (1865–1907). In 1878, the *Tribüne*, another pro-Republican, German-language weekly, began publishing, and though its readership was low at first, it soon became the largest of the German papers. Like most ethnic groups, Germans also had their own social clubs, and they had a lot of them. (Courtesy of IHS.)

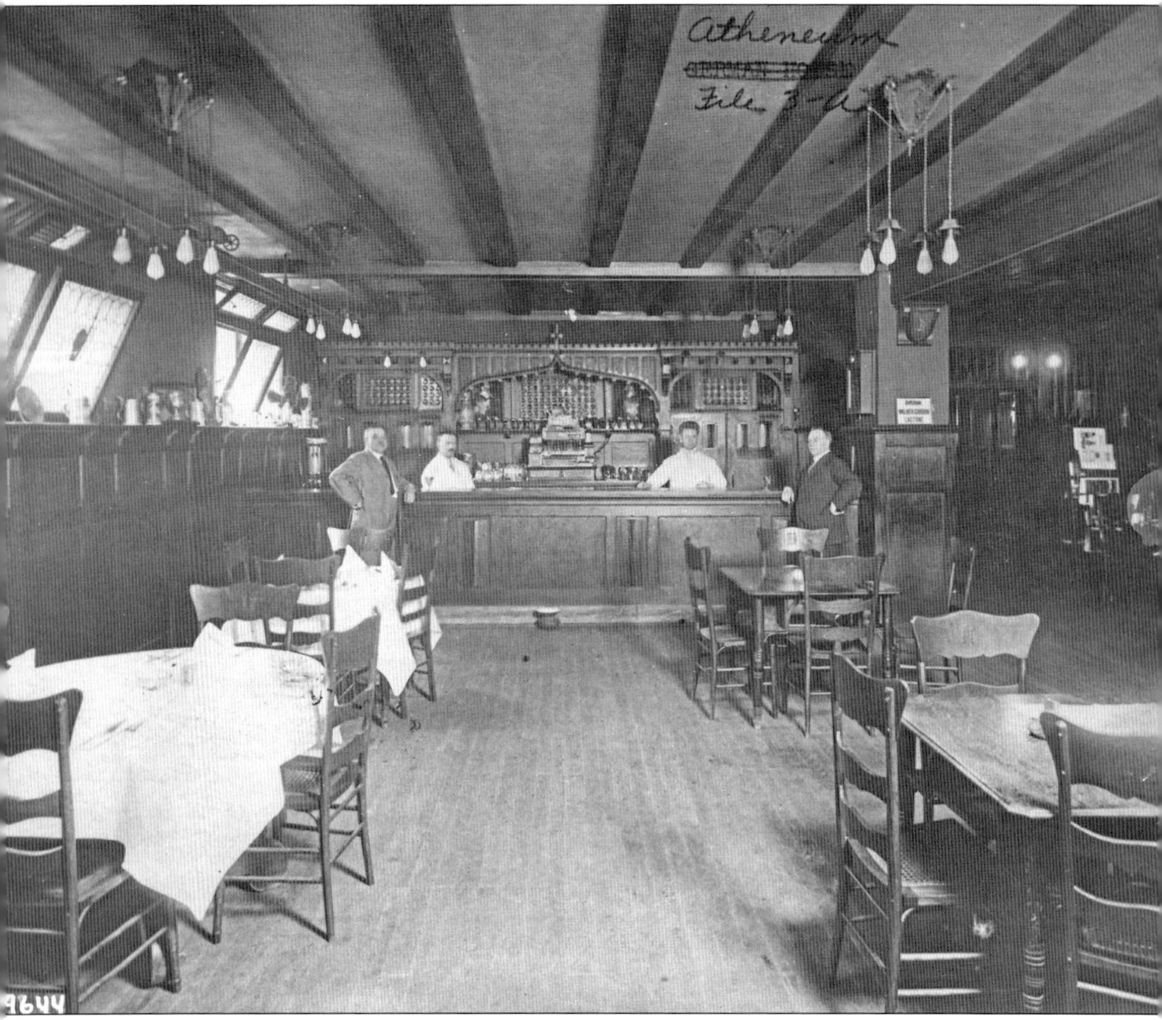

In 1905, Indianapolis had almost 50 clubs dominated by German immigrants, and many of those found a home in Das Deutsche Haus. Since many of these clubs were dominated by Friedenkers, people who had no religious affiliation, they may have served the needs for community and inclusion that would otherwise have been provided by churches. The opening of the west wing in 1898 may be described as the opening chapter in the long history of this venerable building and the culture that it birthed and nurtured. The east wing had opened its doors four years earlier and contained the Rathskeller, the gymnasium, and a *Kegelbahn* (a short, German nine-pin bowling alley), but it was not a true community center without the features that define the building today: the grand theater, the lobby and its magnificent winding staircase, and the largest wall of stained glass in a secular building in Indiana. Both the interior and exterior are magnificent. (Courtesy of the Library of Congress.)

All partners in Vonnegut & Bohn, the architectural firm that designed Das Deutsche Haus, were German-Americans and were trained in both German and American architectural academies. They designed the east wing of Das Deutsche Haus in the German Romanesque style; it was completed in 1893. The west wing, completed in 1897–1898, is a fine example of German Renaisance Revival. The firm's scaled architectural rendering survives and can be found in the Rathskeller today. Newspaper accounts from those days indicate there were initially 300 members of Das Deutsche Haus. Each share of stock was issued for $1,000. (Courtesy of the Library of Congress.)

The group began by building the east wing in 1893–1894, followed by a large west wing in 1897–1898. Vonnegut & Bohn designed both sections. It was the company's first major commission. Vonnegut, together with Arthur Bohn and a later partner, Otto Mueller, also designed schools, churches, department stores, and numerous private homes in Indianapolis. Some of their most noted buildings were the William H. Block Company and the Fletcher Trust Building. One of the wonders of Das Deutsche Haus is that no matter where one looks, there is an architectural gem to intrigue. The devil below sculpted above the fireplace mantle in Das Deutsche Haus's tavern room peers over a passage of dialogue between Mephistopheles and Faust. It is pictured around 1970. (Both, courtesy of the Library of Congress.)

Freidenkers, or free thinkers, were well represented among the Athenaeum's founders and included Clemens Vonnegut. His son Bernard was one of the architects who designed Das Deutsche Haus in 1893. The building, located on Massachusetts Avenue, has 14-foot-high ceilings, a gabled roof, an entrance with semicircular limestone arches flanked by two free-standing Roman Doric columns, and stone lions with shields and lyres. The building contains more stained glass than any other non-ecclesiastical building in Indiana. It is not to be confused with a Catholic or Lutheran church or an Ashkenazi synagogue, as there is no evidence of religious services ever occurring here. Other decorative features include a three-story brick tower with a conical slate roof, arched upper windows, and bullseye gymnasium windows. Social events included costume parties like this one held by the Mueller and Schnull families at the Athenaeum in 1915. (Courtesy of IHS.)

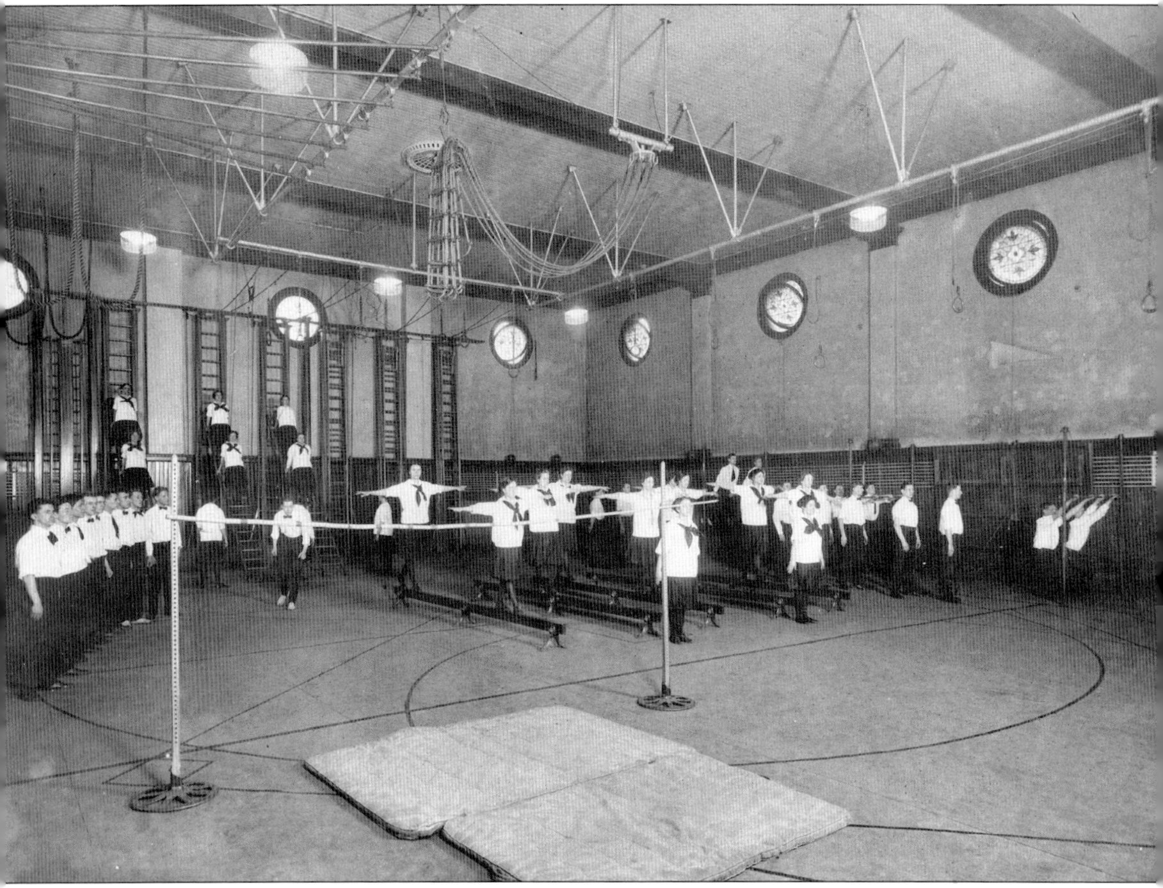

If the name Vonnegut is familiar, Clemens Vonnegut Jr.'s great-grandson was the famous author Kurt Vonnegut. The Vonneguts, a prominent family in Indianapolis, are entwined with the history of Das Deutsche Haus and Indianapolis. Clemens Vonnegut immigrated to America in 1850 and two years later bought a hardware store and turned it into a financial juggernaut. His sons, including Bernard, helped teach gymnastics, and he co-founded the Turnverein. Turnverein were more than just places to practice physical fitness; they were also social and political organizations with a focus on improving health through exercise and healthy living. There were several Turnvereins in Indianapolis, including the Southside Turnverein Club and the Independent Turnverein, also known as the Hoosier Athletic Club. (Courtesy of Bass Photo Co. Collection, IHS.)

One of the dining rooms at the Rathskeller is pictured here, looking very much like the original more than 120 years ago. (Courtesy of Bass Photo Co. Collection, IHS.)

This sign in the Rathskeller reads, "Life is Serious; Art is Delightful." (Courtesy of Athenaeum Foundation.)

The Turnverein was just one of Das Deutsche Haus's many clubs and societies, including the Musikverein, the Lyra, the Damenverein (Ladies' Club), the orchestra, the choir, and of course, the Turners. The Turner movement was a formidable one thanks to its founder, Friedrich Ludwig Jahn. Turner clubs sprang up in every city where significant numbers of German immigrants could be found. Individual members of these societies paid dues, giving them access to the building's facilities and helping fund the building's operating costs. Families would gather for dinner and maybe attend a performance in the grand theater afterwards, perhaps the Athenaeum's house orchestra performing Wagner's *Tannhaeuser* or some other German music. There were also cozy spots for enjoying quiet time with friends. (Courtesy of Bass Photo Co. Collection, IHS.)

Das Deutsche Haus's grand stairway and theater are pictured here in 1910. (Both, courtesy of Bass Photo Co. Collection, IHS.)

One can imagine this scene on a Saturday in spring around 1905, when Das Deutsche Haus was at its zenith. The building would have been throbbing with life, with people in the Rathskeller and Kellerbar (in the west wing atrium) bantering in both English and German, occasionally erupting in explosive laughter. The gymnasium would be echoing with the voices of children and the accented voice of their stern gymnastics instructor. From both the kegelbahnen and American-style bowling alleys would ring a cacophony of laughter, beer glasses clinking, and balls rolling on hardwood and hitting duck pins. The aroma of food would be ubiquitous. Upstairs, the three sumptuously furnished parlor rooms would be packed with ladies—members of the Damenverein—surreptitiously smoking, drinking, and gossiping, confident that their children were in good hands at the gymnasium or children's theater nearby. (Courtesy of Bass Photo Co. Collection, IHS.)

At the Athenaeum, men would be huddled at the Stammtisch drinking good locally brewed German beer or at one of the other grand places in the Athenaeum to enjoy a drink while cementing business deals. Outside, an orchestra would be playing to a packed biergarten. Perhaps there would be a wedding reception going on in an east-wing room as well. The building consumed a quarter of a city block, a massive footprint that equals that of the city's major skyscrapers today. The walled-in biergarten included a band shell that survives to this day, designed to focus music from bands and orchestras in the days before electronic amplification. Dan Wakefield, author of *Going All the Way*, hails from Indy, and a scene from the movie based on his book was filmed at the biergarten. (Courtesy of the Library of Congress.)

A grand and spacious place, Das Deutsche Haus was built to last many generations, with limestone and brick masonry and a cavernous, and very steep, slate hipped roof crowned with dormers, cupolas, and architectural details typical of both the German Romanesque and Renaissance Revival architectural styles. Unfortunately, as the building neared completion, money became tight. To economize, the founders resorted to a new, and unproven, building material that possessed the malleability of copper but not its durability: galvanized steel. From the ground, the building's roof upon its completion looked to be the equal of any seen in Europe. It must have invoked a bit of *Heimweh* (homesickness). Unfortunately, the cost savings from that substitution of materials would later prove to be fool's gold. (Courtesy of the Library of Congress.)

To a 21st-century observer, this might seem a convoluted arrangement of clubs within clubs. But to 19th-century German immigrants, club membership was a defining part of life as well as a badge of identity, and it all got sorted out over beer. Less than 10 years after it opened, membership had swelled to over 800 people. This inclusive community center hosted programs for the enrichment, education, and enjoyment of men, women, and children. Race and ethnicity in most cases didn't matter, but men and women had their own organizations and rooms in which to congregate. The west wing ladies' parlor is pictured above around 1898. Below, the grand staircase is still a major feature of the Athenaeum. (Both, courtesy of Bass Photo Co. Collection, IHS.)

Jack Adams and his band are pictured at the Maennerchor, founded by German immigrants in 1854. At the time of their final performance in 2018, they had been performing continuously for 164 years. (Courtesy of IHS.)

An article in the *Indianapolis Journal* on Friday, August 17, 1900, titled "A Torchlight Parade Will Inaugurate the Celebration of German Day" lists an amazing number of German clubs, societies, and bands, including the Cherusker Lodge Harugari and such societies as the Bavarian, Badischea, Prussian, Pfaeizer, Alpha, Herman, Springdal, German-American Mutual Aid, Harmonia, Germania, and Heimath; bands from societies such as the German Pioneer, German Butchers, Schwaben, Low German, Southside Schwaben, Sachen, and Knights of St. George; and German Smoking Casino No. 1. Other music groups included the Lyra and Musikverein. Many of these clubs, including Das Deutsche Haus, had restaurants, performing halls, and casual dining areas. The Maennerchor Hall, pictured here, was built in 1907. (Courtesy of Ronald Flick.)

The 18th Amendment and the Volstead Act that enforced it outlawed—but did not prevent—the "manufacture, sale or transportation of intoxicating liquors." The Athenaeum, as it was now called, was still a place where one could find drink (as was the Maennerchor, pictured above in 1908), though patrons were a bit less brazen about it. Those who could afford it hoarded it while they could, and private cellars and clubs were well stocked by January 16, 1920. The Volstead Act allowed alcohol to be purchased for medicinal purposes, and within six months of its enactment, 15,000 doctors and 57,000 pharmacists had obtained licenses to prescribe medicinal alcohol. Grape juice remained unrestricted, and output quadrupled, often sold in kits with dire warnings that the juice would ferment into wine if allowed to sit for 60 days and with specific instructions on how to avoid just that. (Above, courtesy of Bass Photo Co. Collection, IHS; right, courtesy of Indiana Landmarks.)

The Kniepe (drinking room) on the second floor of the Maennerchor building is seen here. Unique because of its eclectic combination of German and American stylistic detailing, the Maennerchor was located at 102 West Michigan Street. (Courtesy of the Library of Congress.)

In 1854, a small group of German immigrants formed an all-male choir called the Maennerchor and started performing at Washington Hall and other downtown venues. By 1878, the club needed more space to accommodate its growing membership. Impressive performances drew loud, large crowds, and the Maennerchor flourished in the Indianapolis community. According to Historic Indiana, the Maennechor's 1904 golden jubilee was a three-day festival that included the gift of a special gold medal from Kaiser Wilhelm of Germany. During the presentation, which occurred during a banquet featuring—of course—foods from the Fatherland, celebrants rose to their feet and raised their glasses, shouting "Hock der Kaiser." It was a very German evening. But glory does not last forever; the Maennerchor was razed in 1974 to make way for an insurance company. The Maennerchor's dining room is seen here. (Courtesy of the Library of Congress.)

There were numerous Turnvereins. The Independent later became the Hoosier Athletic Club and is now an apartment complex. (Courtesy of Bass Photo Co. Collection, IHS.)

The gymnasium at the Independent Turnverein is pictured here in 1914. In 1851, two Turner clubs were founded in Indianapolis. (Courtesy of Bass Photo Co. Collection, IHS.)

The swimming pool at the Independent Turnverein is pictured here in 1914. (Courtesy of Bass Photo Co. Collection, IHS.)

Two

GOOD TIMES, GERMAN STYLE

The golden anniversary of Indianapolis's Mannerchor was observed in 1904. (Courtesy of Ronald Flick.)

The Bundesfest was quite an extravaganza, attracting large crowds of both Germans and others. According to the *Plymouth Tribune* of June 1, 1905, "When the Bundes Turnfest is held at Indianapolis June 21-25, thousands of the visitors, no doubt, will visit one of the show pieces of the Hoosier capital [the Soldier's and Sailor's Monument]. . . . The gathering will be under the auspices of the Nord Amerikanischer Turner Bund and 2000 athletes from all parts of the United States will take part. The Deutsche Turnerschaft will be represented by a team of twenty young men, the pick of the German turners." (Courtesy of Ronald Flick.)

This postcard image of the 29th North American Bundesfest in Indianapolis in 1905 reads, "greetings from the festival place." The military style of the camp reflects the plans of some German immigrants of the time to return to Germany and again push for a German republic. (Courtesy of Ronald Flick.)

The Soldier's and Sailor's Monument in Monument Circle was designed by German architect Bruno Schmitz and stands only 15 feet shorter than the Statue of Liberty. Arguably the most recognized landmark in the city, the monument is crowned by a statue that appropriately faces south, where Confederate brigadier general John Hunt Morgan famously brought the fighting onto Hoosier soil in 1863. The monument is also a place to celebrate for city residents and visitors. Listed in the National Register of Historic Places and part of the Washington Street–Monument Circle Historic District, it was the site of the 1905 Indianapolis Turnfest Parade. This photograph shows a parade lining up on Meridian Street, including the Turnverein drum corps. The statue of the running man symbolizes fitness and exercise. (Courtesy of IHS.)

The 1905 Turnfest in Indianapolis, at the height of the organization's glory days, is seen here. (Courtesy of IHS.)

Das Deutsche haus is pictured on this postcard during the Bundesfest des Nord-Americk. (Courtesy of Bass Photo Co. Collection, IHS.)

This crowd on West Market Street was attending the Sangerfest parade. (Courtesy of IHS.)

The German community of Indianapolis certainly loved an extravaganza. In 1908, the National Saengenfest of the North American Saegerbund began its celebration in the morning. At 3:00

p.m., they reassembled for speeches and a parade at Monument Circle. (Courtesy of Ronald Flick.)

This was a souvenier of the Saengerfest musical festival held in Indianapolis in 1908. Apart from a brief welcome in English, the entire proceedings were carried out in German. (Courtesy of the Ruth Lily Special Collections and Archives, Indiana University–Purdue University Indianapolis.)

The North American Saengerbund banner was on display, carried on a float drawn by six white horses. Aboard the float, a statuesque woman representing Germania was surrounded by young men and women. A concert was held that night at Indiana State Fairgrounds Coliseum. (Creative Commons.)

US vice president Charles W. Fairbanks, who is buried in Crown Hill Cemetery and was a member of the Indianapolis Maennerchor, spoke along with Indianapolis banker John P. Frenzel, who served as the treasurer of the North American Saengerbund. Overall, the festival attracted 75,000 visitors to the city and was instrumental in establishing Indianapolis as a national center for German culture in America. (Courtesy of Ronald Flick.)

Three

The Neighborhood and Beyond

Standing sentinel for well over a century, Das Deutsche Haus is located in Indianapolis's trendy Massachusetts Avenue, a place of eclectic shops, restaurants, and art galleries as well as a stop on the city's cultural trail. But the neighborhood is tethered to the past as well, with a showcase of historic buildings. The Athenaeum is located within Lockerbie Square Historic District, a delightful collection of Italianate, Federal, and Queen Anne homes as well as smaller bungalows dating even further back to when the neighborhood was called Germantown because of the number of German immigrants who lived there. The majority of the homes in Lockerbie Square were built in the mid- to late 1800s. Once considered a suburb, it is close to the heart of downtown. (Courtesy of Bass Photo Co. Collection, IHS.)

The best known resident of Lockerbie was James Whitcomb Riley, the internationally acclaimed Hoosier known for such poems as "The Old Swimming Hole" and "Little Orphan Annie." (Courtesy of the Library of Congress.)

First titled "The Elf Child" when he wrote the poem in 1885, Riley later changed the title to "Little Orphan Annie." Annie was probably really Mary Alice "Allie" Smith, a neighbor of the Riley family who came to live with them when her father was killed during the Civil War. Like Annie in the poem, Allie (a typo in the original text was the reason she is called Annie in the poem) liked to frighten the other children with her spooky stories. Riley was so impressed that he remembered those scary evenings decades later. This 1900 photograph taken by Elizabeth Brownell was used to illustrate Riley's poem. (Courtesy of the Library of Congress.)

Riley lived in this home for 23 years but never owned it. He moved here in 1893 at the apex of his career, sharing the house with the Nickum and Holstein families. Located at 528 Lockerbie Street, the home was designated a national historic landmark and offers visitors a glimpse into the life of the great "Hoosier Poet." These interior views, both then and now, show the typical heavy hand of Victorian decor. (Above, courtesy of the Library of Congress; below, courtesy of Visit Indy.)

Now a house museum, the James Whitcomb Riley Home was built in 1872 in the Italianate style. When Riley died in 1916, his friends created the Riley Memorial Association with the purpose of starting a children's hospital in the city, since none then existed. The Riley Hospital opened in 1924 and is now the Riley Children's Foundation. It includes the home and Billie Lou Wood Visitor Center, Camp Riley for children with physical disabilities in Martinsville, Indiana, and Riley Hospital for Children, one of the premier children's research hospitals in the world. (Courtesy of Visit Indy.)

It is not known for sure if Riley hung out at the Athenaeum's Biergarten, Rathskeller, or Kellerbar (above), but he certainly liked to have a drink or two (or more), and it was just a short walk away. There is a story that Riley once over-imbibed at the Germania House, now the Slippery Noodle and one of the oldest bars in the state, having opened before 1851. He was walking home when he became so tired that he laid down and fell asleep. He awoke to find himself in a pumpkin patch; this became the inspiration for one of his most famous poems, "When the Frost is on the Punkin." Surely, the many youngsters who listened to this wonderful paean to the beauty of nature written by the man nicknamed the "Children's Poet" had no idea it came about after a drunken binge. (Above, courtesy of IHS; below, courtesy of the Library of Congress.)

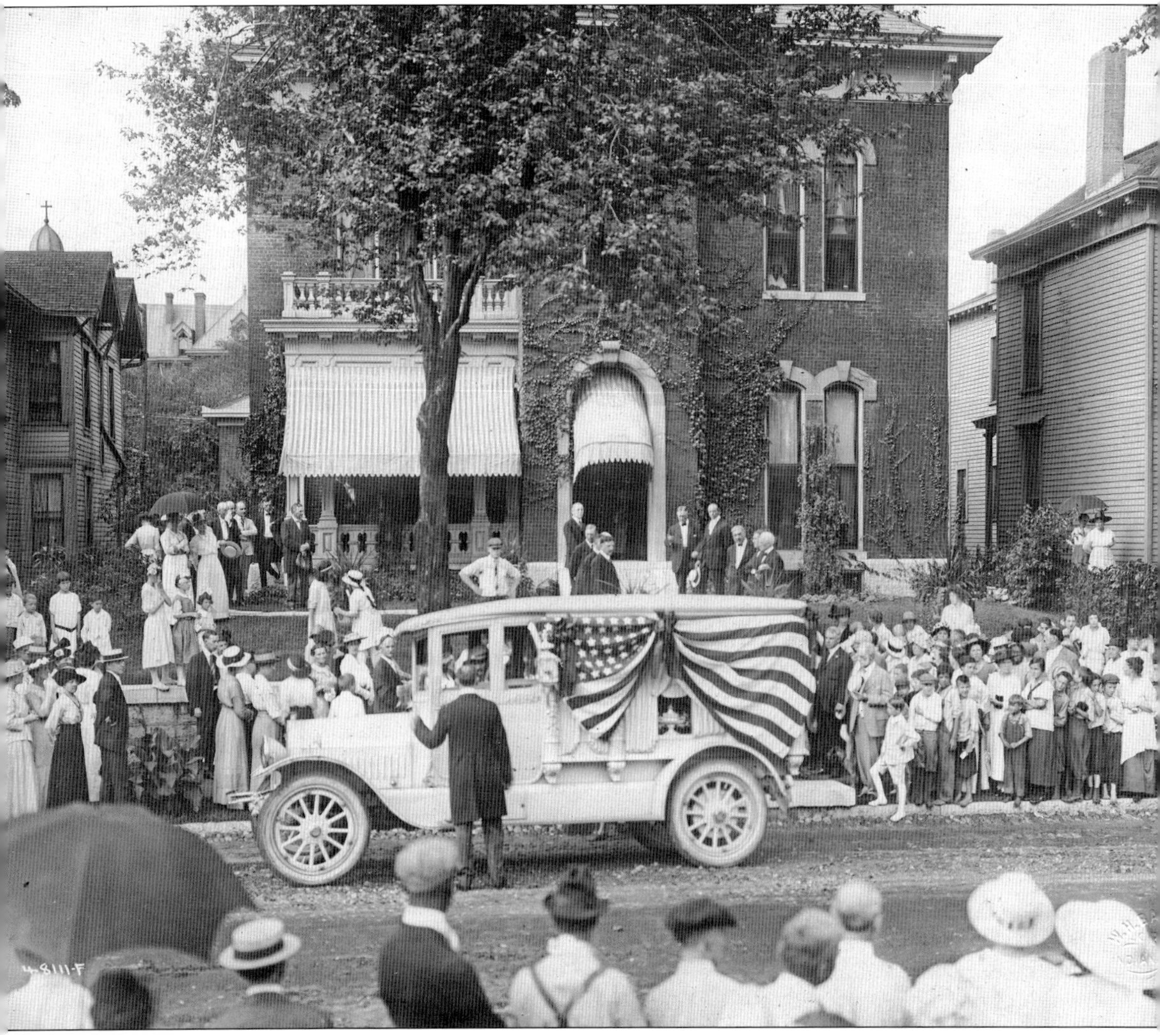

In 1865, Abraham Lincoln's funeral train was the first to pass through Indianapolis; James Whitcomb Riley's was the second in 1916. More than 35,000 mourners came to pay their respects. (Courtesy of Bass Photo Co. Collection, IHS.)

The James Whitcomb Riley memorial at Crown Hill Cemetery in Indianapolis is seen here. (Courtesy of Marty N. Davis.)

These bas reliefs from the Germantown Monument show "The Volunteer" at left and "Protest against Slavery" below. (Both, courtesy of Indiana Landmarks.)

The Zion United Church of Christ located on New Jersey Avenue and North Street was founded in 1841 by Evangelical Lutherans who had immigrated from Germany. Services were held in their native language. The structure shown in this 1914 photograph was designed by D.A. Bohlen and built the year before. (Courtesy of Bass Photo Co. Collection, IHS.)

Most of the homes in Lockerbie Square were built from the mid- to late 1800s. Once considered a suburb, it was close to the heart of downtown. The photograph above shows one of the smaller homes in the neighborhood. One of the best neighborhoods in Indianapolis, Lockerbie Square is a charming step back into time, its homes, both large and small, have been lovingly restored. (Above, courtesy of Indiana Landmarks; below, courtesy of Jim Grey.)

Still an anchor on Massachusetts Avenue, the Murat Shrine Center is as elaborate as the Athenaeum in architectural style. Over the years it has been the site of much entertainment, as seen in the photograph below. (Above, courtesy of Visit Indy; below, courtesy of Library of Congress.)

Located diagonally across from Das Deutsche Haus on the corners of North and New Jersey Streets is another amazing building now known as the Old National Centre. Built in 1910, the 130,379-square-foot building was the 17th Temple of the Ancient Arabic Order of the Nobles of the Mystic Shrine, then later by less grandiose names such as the Murat Shrine Temple and the Murat Shrine Center. Moorish in design, it is distinctive with stained-glass windows, terra-cotta trim, brown and yellow brick banding, and a roofline featuring a 209-foot tower and minarets. (Both, courtesy of the Library of Congress.)

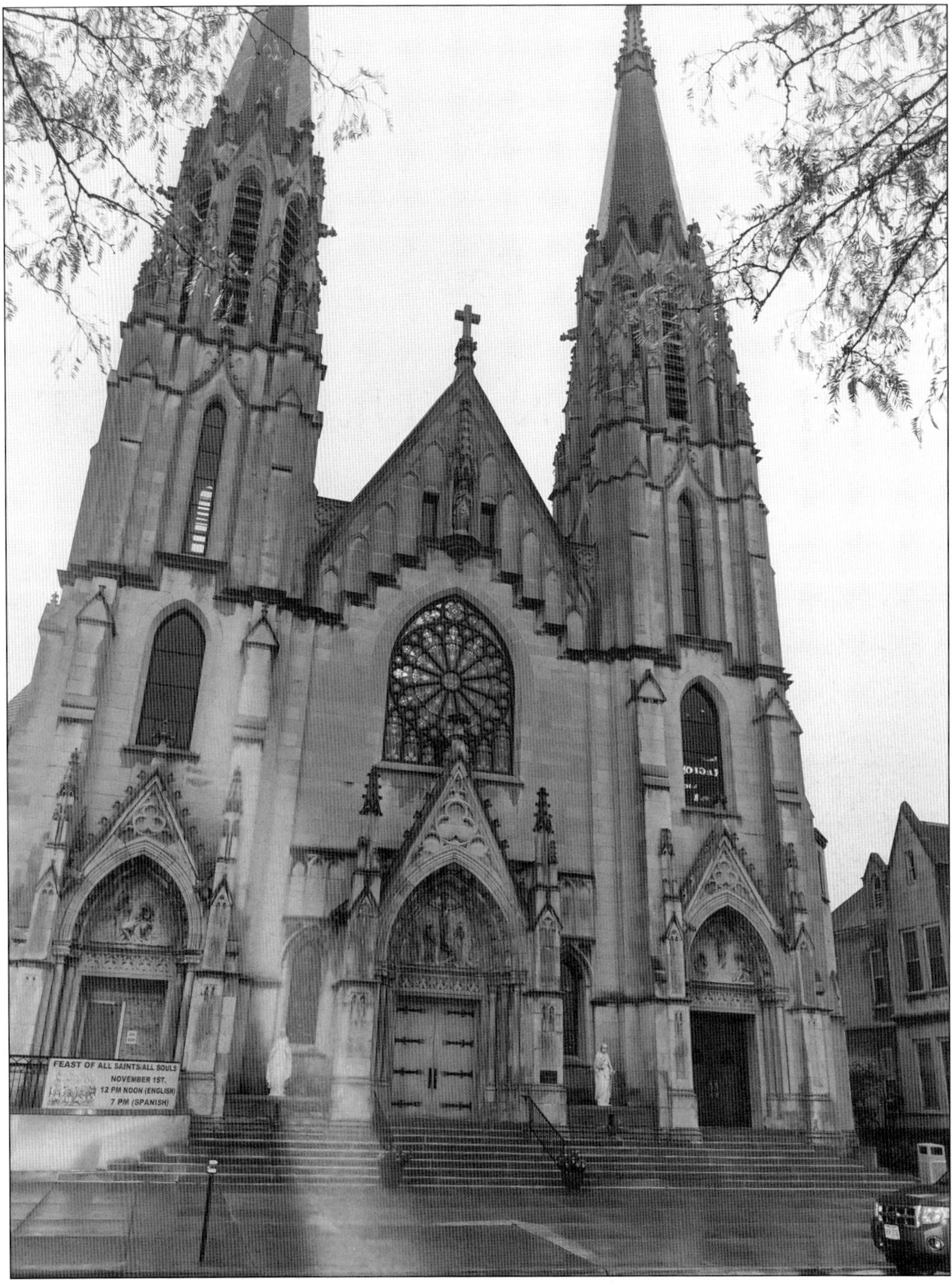

Even older than the Athenaeum, another longtime survivor is St. Mary's Catholic Church (originally St. Marienkirche), which has been serving the Lockerbie neighborhood and immigrant community, including Germans, since 1858. It still stands tall near the Athenaeum. (Jane Simon Ammeson.)

Four

The Athenaeum Impact

The current resurgence of craft beer often relies upon the recipes and history of local breweries, and Indianapolis had more than its share, some 90 percent owned by Germans, many of whom were members of the Athenaeum. According to Bob Ostrander, coauthor of the excellent *Hoosier Beer: Tapping into Indiana Brewing History*, Peter Lieber, a native of Duesseldorf, Germany, who came to the United States at the age of 18 and served in the Union army, was the brother of Herman Lieber, founding member of Das Deutsche Haus. The two, along with Charles Mayer, opened P. Lieber Brewing Company (City Brewing) and made Tafel, Würzburger Style, Special Brew, Olden Time Ale, Porter, and Hoosier Beer. (Courtesy of IHS.)

C.F. Schmidt's Brewery was founded by Christian Frederick Schmidt and Charles Jaeger, who a year later sold his interest, believing Schmidt's ideas were, according to Ostrander, too grandiose to succeed. Schmidt, a German immigrant, built a two-story brewhouse with a brick icehouse and a large cellar. Later would come stables, a malting house, and a bottling plant, creating a sprawling facility that spread across a full city block at McCarty and Alabama Streets. The area is now part of the Eli Lily complex. Schmidt's beer was extremely popular with Germans, who liked its authentic taste. Their brands were Bock, Budweiser, Cream Ale, Dublin Porter, Export, Stock Ale, and Tonica. (Courtesy of IHS.)

Numerous breweries, including Schmidt's, P. Lieber, and C. Maus Brewery, merged into the Indianapolis Brewing Company (IBC), founded in 1887. Each continued its own brewing operations. Located on Madison Avenue at Parkway Avenue, P. Lieber became the main brewery for the company. The innovative company had rail service, making shipment of IBC beer throughout the state easy. Albert Lieber was the company's second president. In an Athenaeum connection, he was the maternal grandfather of Kurt Vonnegut Jr. Lieber's daughter Edith married Kurt Vonnegut Sr., who was a successful architect like his father, Bernard. In another connection to Das Deutsche Haus, Kurt Sr.'s mother, Nannie Schnull Vonnegut, was the daughter of Henry Schnull, one of the Athenaeum's founders. (Courtesy of Bass Photo Co. Collection, IHS.)

These tunnels leading from Schmidt's Brewery on McCarty Street were used to store beer before refrigeration was readily available. At one time, Indianapolis had 18 breweries. (Courtesy of IHS.)

Col. Richard H. Lieber, shown here, was the nephew of Herman Lieber, the art patron and founding member of Das Deutsche Haus. Colonel Lieber helped to found Indiana's state park system. A successful businessman and dedicated conservationist, he was the first director of the Indiana Department of Conservation. In this 1918 photograph, he is wearing his military dress uniform, as he served in World War I as Gov. James Goodrich's military secretary as well as a liaison between Indiana and the US War Department. The Liebers were high in the social strata of Indianapolis and immensely rich, their fortune based on the production of beer. (Courtesy of Bretzman Collection, IHS.)

By 1877, local interest in art had grown, and two Indiana artists who had studied in Europe opened an art school. When T.C. Steele, who would become famous for his landscapes of Brown County, wanted to study art in Europe, Herman Lieber devised a plan to finance the trip for Steele and his family to stay in Munich, raising an initial $1,300. During Steele's overseas stay, which lasted from 1880 to 1885, he sent Lieber and other sponsors copies of paintings from the art galleries in Munich as well as his own original works. The H. Lieber & Company Art Emporium is pictured here. (Courtesy of IHS.)

Deutschen Allgemeinnen Protestantischen Waisenvereins (German General Protestant Orphan Association), later known as the Pleasant Run Children's Home, was designed by architect Diedrich A. Bohlen. Built in 1871–1872, it accommodated about 50 children. The name was changed from the German in 1918. Below, children at the orphanage enjoy dinner. (Both, courtesy of Ronald Flick.)

Founded in 1911 by German American Harry Clayton Stutz, the Stutz Moto Car Company manufactured sports and luxury cars at its Indianapolis plant. Growing up on a farm in Ansonia, Ohio, but determined that the farming life was not for him, Harry Stutz began tinkering with making a car out of castoff agricultural parts such as a binder chain and a stationary gasoline engine. Though not a high performer, "Old Hickory" (as he called it) was able to move both forwards and backwards. At the time, the idea of going backwards was revolutionary, since a horse by nature would not run backwards. Stutz made its racing debut at the Indianapolis 500 on May 10, 1911. The title of the photograph below is "Stutz Wrecked." (Above, courtesy of the IHS; below, courtesy of the Library of Congress.)

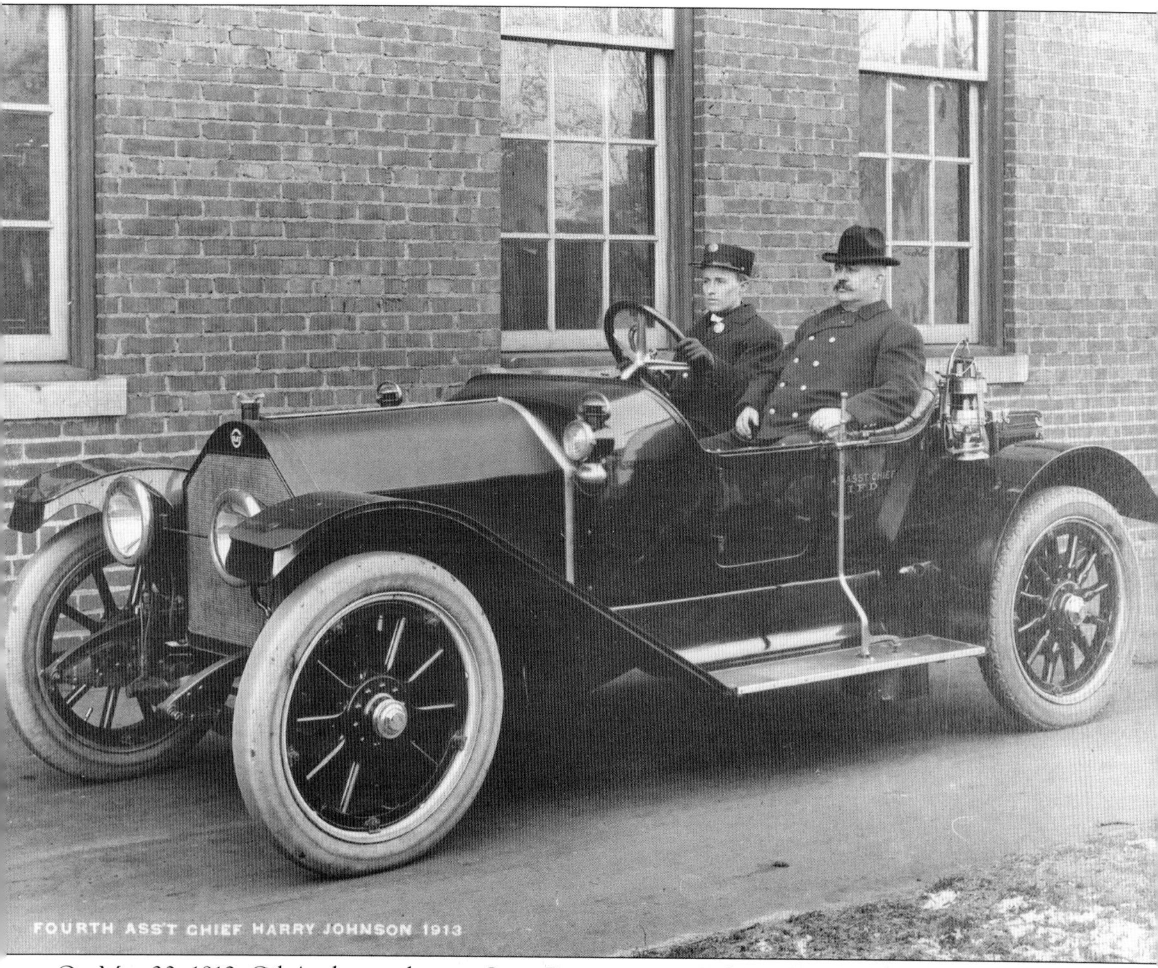

On May 30, 1912, Gil Andersen drove a Stutz Bearcat racer at the Indianapolis 500 Mile Race, but an accident on turn three kept him from finishing. Len Zengel finished the race in another Stutz machine, coming in sixth. Carl Fisher drove the pace car—another Stutz. At the company's zenith, the car was so popular that even the Indianapolis fire chief rode in one, as seen here. Unfortunately, Stutz Motor Company went out of business in 1935. (Courtesy of IHS.)

Fisher, joined by another Hoosier entrepreneur, James Allison, promoted the idea of building the nation's first transcontinental highway. Their goal was to enable 25,000 automobile tourists to drive to the Panama-Pacific Exposition in 1915. On September 10, 1912, the two announced their project at Das Deutsche Haus in front of a group of automobile and accessory manufacturers who had been invited to Indianapolis for the announcement. It was a success. Not only did Fisher raise $1 million in pledges, but the project also received national attention. Little is left of that highway, though markers commemorate it. Ultimately, it would change the way Americans traveled. (Both, courtesy of IHS.)

Carl G. Fisher was one of the major investors in the Indianapolis Motor Speedway and manufacturer of Prest-O-Lite carbide-gas headlights, found on most automobiles throughout the country (before his invention, car lights were basically lanterns). He believed that if cars were the future of America, then Americans needed good roads to drive on. His idea was to create a transcontinental highway connecting Times Square in New York City to Lincoln Park in San Francisco, a route traversing 13 states, 128 counties, and over 700 villages, towns, and cities. Because Abraham Lincoln was his hero—and because Fisher was a great marketer—he proposed calling it the Lincoln Highway. By the 1920s, deliveries made by horse and wagon such as the one above for the Indianapolis Brewing Company were almost obsolete, being replaced by delivery trucks such as the one below for K.W. Klemm Sausage . The company, owned by Karl and Mina Klemm, opened in 1913; now owned by a family member, it is today Claus' German Sausage & Meats. (Above, courtesy of Bass Photo Co. Collection, IHS; below, courtesy of Klemm family, IHS.)

Kurt Vonnegut Jr. famously said, "All my jokes are Indianapolis. All my attitudes are Indianapolis. My adenoids are Indianapolis. If I ever severed myself from Indianapolis, I would be out of business. What people like about me is Indianapolis." The Vonnegut Room at the Athenaeum is dedicated to the family and what they did for Das Deutsche Haus and the city. The Vonnegut hardware store was in business from 1852 to 1965. Originally it was a one-room store where merchandise was stacked on the wooden sidewalk fronting the building. It offered animal hides, dry goods, groceries, coffin fittings, and supplies for butchering, harness-making, carpentry, and farming. Because roads were rudimentary and travel difficult, the owners served cheese, crackers, and Madison ale—considered one of the finest of its time and brewed in Madison, Indiana—to weary shoppers. (Courtesy of Bass Photo Co. Collection, IHS.)

The Vonnegut Hardware building is a reminder of the forces that initially helped build the Athenaeum. The restoration of the Athenaeum shows the changes that have come about since the McCray bill made it illegal to teach German in schools during World War I (it was lifted in 1923). But there was much to be done. The Athenaeum had become dingy and suffered from a lack of maintenance. Though the building possessed a durable slate roof, the pins holding that slate, as well as its soffits and dormers, were made of galvanized steel, not copper. Within a century of the Athenaeum's construction, the steel had decomposed, sometimes unleashing a landslide of slate shingles onto the sidewalk. Corroded dormers allowed water and pigeons to enter the building. By 1991, there was at least a foot of guano in the Athenaeum's attic. Dusty guano is a human health hazard and is highly combustible, and pigeons are sometimes known to hoard lit cigarette butts. Athena was definitely looking after the building during those years. (Courtesy of Bass Photo Co. Collection, IHS.)

Germans provided Indianapolis with culture, civic responsibility, and, because of their successes in business, jobs at places like the Vonnegut hardware store. The store was in business for more than a century. (Both, courtesy of Bass Photo Co. Collection, IHS.)

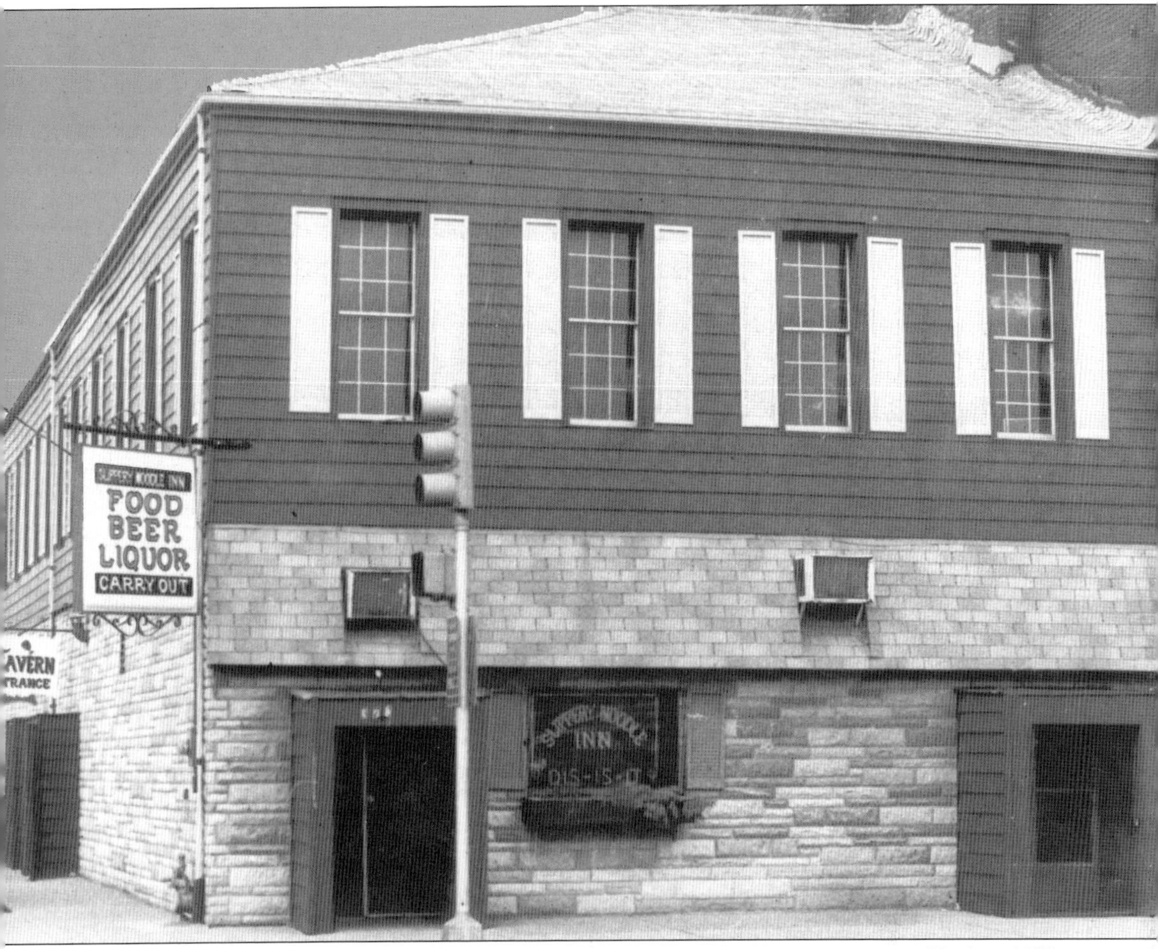

The Slippery Noodle Inn was owned by various German immigrants since it opened before 1850. It is the oldest bar in Indiana. It has had many names, including Germania, the name of the first ship to bring Germans to America. Like other Freethinkers, the original owner had the building designed to harbor freedom seekers traveling on the Underground Railroad. It is said to be haunted by one of the escaped slaves who stayed behind to help other slaves find freedom. (Courtesy of the Slippery Noodle.)

Students at Charles E. Emmerich Manual Training High School in Indianapolis are pictured on Ivy Day in 1923. In 1909, the principal Mr. Emmerich started the tradition of planting a sprig of ivy along the west wall of the school; by 1952, the entire side of the building was covered. It was not an uncommon tradition in Indiana schools during that time. (Courtesy of IHS.)

The classical Renaissance Revival style Indiana Statehouse, made of Indiana limestone, was completed in 1888 and is a centerpiece of the city's downtown. (Courtesy of Library of Congress.)

Reminders of German architects, landscape artists, and sculptors such as Bolen, Vonnegut, and Scherrer can be seen throughout Indianapolis, including in the Crown Hill Cemetery. The magnificent cemetery, with over 200,000 graves, is listed in the National Register of Historic Places. Originally, omnibuses and steam-powered boats along the Central Canal took visitors to the cemetery. Cars were not allowed until 1912. (Courtesy of the Library of Congress.)

Five

The Retreat of Reason

German-language newspapers in Indiana and elsewhere reacted in horror to the sinking of the *Lusitania* by a U-boat in 1915, and the news was on the lips of everyone in the Rathskeller. For the most part, newly arrived German immigrants loved their adopted home, and their loyalty to America was never in question. But soon American public opinion shifted dramatically, and Americans of German extraction felt the brunt of it. German-language newspapers in America began to fold. A state law was passed banning the German language from being taught in the public schools—it was rescinded in 1923. Despite winning the war, as seen in this photograph of Red Cross nurses at Monument Circle celebrating the unconfirmed peace on November 7, 1918, xenophobia spread. (Courtesy of IHS.)

World War I was followed by Prohibition. It didn't help that America was being flooded with emigrants from Germany, Ireland, and Italy, places in which alcohol was accepted as an important part of daily life. Germans in particular sought to meet this demand and quickly established

breweries in every major Midwestern city. All this fit in with stereotypes of foreigners. Breweries started to close; fortunes and jobs were lost. The passage of Prohibition, despite its unpopularity, seemed more and more unlikely. (Courtesy of the Library of Congress.)

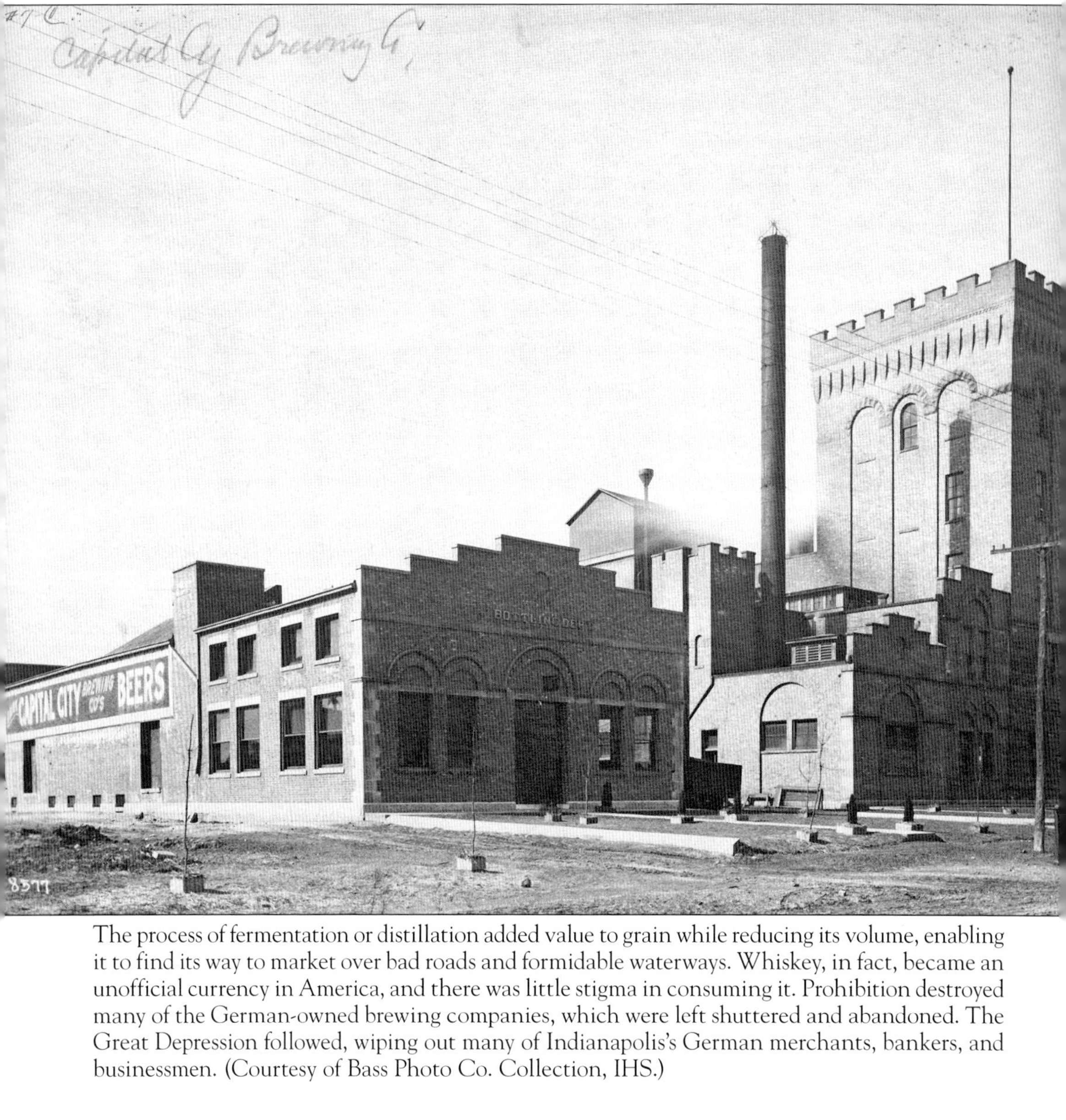

The process of fermentation or distillation added value to grain while reducing its volume, enabling it to find its way to market over bad roads and formidable waterways. Whiskey, in fact, became an unofficial currency in America, and there was little stigma in consuming it. Prohibition destroyed many of the German-owned brewing companies, which were left shuttered and abandoned. The Great Depression followed, wiping out many of Indianapolis's German merchants, bankers, and businessmen. (Courtesy of Bass Photo Co. Collection, IHS.)

The Athenaeum, stripped of its cultural identity, hemorrhaged members. Those who remained were old and viewed as anachronistic. The Athenaeum's Turner Club, and for that matter the Turner movement in general, withered. People were happy to join the YMCA or fitness centers in the suburbs instead. The old Normal College of the North American Gymnastics Union that had occupied the Athenaeum since 1907 vacated in 1970 and metamorphosized into the Department of Physical Education at Indiana University–Purdue University Indianapolis (IUPUI). The South Side Turnverein, a grand building designed by Vonnegut & Bohn to serve much the same purpose as the Athenaeum, still stands, divided from the corporate campus of Eli Lilly & Company by the eight-lane Interstate 70. The Athenaeum was falling into shambles. (Both, courtesy of Indiana Landmarks.)

Then another, even more horrific, war was fought with Germany. By the time the Red Army had liberated Hitler's death camps on its way to Berlin, it had become decidedly unfashionable to be German, even for those, like Kurt Vonnegut, who had fought against the odious Nazi regime. Those were very dark days for the Athenaeum, and generally for Germans in America. The National Prohibition Convention was held in Indianapolis. Prohibition resulted in the closing of many of the breweries and the loss of many jobs as well as fortunes. (Both, courtesy of Bass Photo Co. Collection, IHS.)

Almost half a million Hoosiers belonged to the Ku Klux Klan during the 1920s. During that decade, Ed Jackson, a known member of the Klan, was elected governor of the state. There was also an affiliated organization called Women of the Ku Klux Klan. The Grand Dragon of the Klan lived in the beautiful Irvington section of Indianapolis until his arrest and conviction in the brutal rape and subsequent death of Marge Oberholtzer. Edwards was not re-elected. This chilling photograph shows the Klan attending a funeral. But the return to reason was taking hold. (Courtesy of the Huntington Historical Society.)

The Ku Klux Klan is shown here at a gathering at Ridgelawn Cemetery in 1925. (Courtesy of the Calumet Regional Archives, Indiana University Northwest.)

The German Freethinkers were staunch abolitionists. It was their determination as well as that of many others that helped rid Indiana of the KKK. (Courtesy of the Library of Congress.)

World War I, Prohibition, the Depression, and then World War II—all of these changes sweeping America had enormous and lasting consequences for the Athenaeum. People migrated en masse from old urban neighborhoods into new suburbs serviced by supermarkets and strip malls. The automobile became king of the road, and commuting became common. The core of Indianapolis, and a great many other American cities, began to die. Germans and other ethnic groups had tried so hard to blend in that their children no longer had as much interest in clubs and social organizations catering to the traditions of their parents' or grandparents' native lands. Beautiful buildings declined and were lost as neighborhoods and lifestyles changed. (Both, courtesy of Indiana Landmarks.)

In the late 1980s, the local fire marshal threatened to shutter the Athenaeum unless it constructed a fire escape from the theater. The massive, and shedding, asbestos theater curtain was not up to the task of protecting the public from a major fire, and there was only one escape route—the main steps. Unable to raise the necessary funds from members, the Turners borrowed $70,000 from Historic Landmarks Foundation of Indiana Inc., a preservation organization loath to see the building abandoned. The Historic Landmarks Foundation took a mortgage on the building to secure the loan, and though the Turners built the fire escape, they never paid a dime back. Thus, for a decade or more, the Athenaeum's only mortgage was in default. (Both, courtesy of Indiana Landmarks.)

The Turners soldiered on, as did the Rathskeller in the Athenaeum's basement, until 1991, when the situation became critical. The cavernous building was no model of fuel efficiency, and its heat source—steam from Indianapolis Power & Light Company piped from the street—was shut off in June for nonpayment. This did not trouble the Turners much until the weather again turned cold. All this was a sign that significant change was needed. (Both, courtesy of Indiana Landmarks.)

In the early 1990s, squatters discovered the vulnerable Athenaeum. Employees gathered every painting, statue, and other tempting object and locked them in hidden storage for safekeeping, but much of value was lost. (Both, courtesy of Indiana Landmarks.)

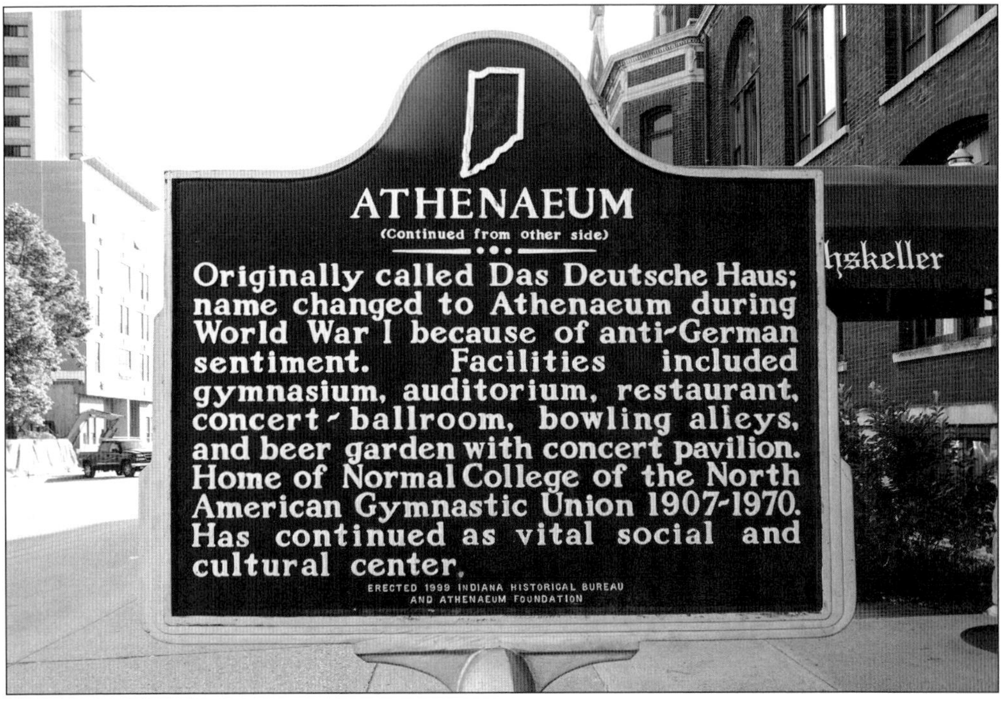

Madame C.J. Walker, the first child in her family born into freedom after Abraham Lincoln signed the Emancipation Proclamation, not only pioneered hair care but also was an automobile buff. Though she had a chauffeur, she liked to drive. She also owned a Waverly electric car, which was claimed by the manufacturer to be easily driven "by women of refinement, without coachman, chauffeur or escort." (Courtesy of Wikimedia.)

It was one fine mess. Freezing temperatures savaged plumbing in the venerable old building, not to mention presenting an inconvenience to the Rathskeller's few remaining customers, or the Turner's few remaining gymnastics students. During these darkest days, amazingly, the Rathskeller retained a small but loyal group of aged German-speaking customers, who would occupy the Stammtisch and pretend that nothing was wrong. When it was time for a vote, the ayes carried the day, and the stockholders of the Socialier Turnverein Aktiengesellschaft adjourned for the final time, some lingering over beer until the complementary keg of Warsteiner had run out. Once the vote was hand delivered to the Marion County Recorder's Office, the Athenaeum Foundation, on paper at least, had become the owner of the Athenaeum. (Courtesy of Indiana Landmarks.)

Six

Honoring the Past and Embracing the Future

It is said that success has many fathers, but failure is an orphan. When it became obvious to outsiders that the Athenaeum was in new and capable hands, help began to arrive from a great many sources. (Courtesy of Indiana Landmarks.)

One of the board's first challenges was to get the building's heat turned back on. Indianapolis Power & Light Company, not much inclined to civic generosity, refused to do so unless presented with a $25,000 check. A call to Crystal DeHaan, a German immigrant who owned Resort Condominiums International Inc., one of the city's most prominent businesses, resulted in her sending a check by courier later that afternoon. And there were lights! When the Athenaeum Foundation's application for recognition of tax-exempt status became bogged down in bureaucratic red tape, Hofstetter solved that problem with one phone call to Sen. Richard G. Lugar. A call from the IRS to Hofstetter soon followed informing him of the good news that tax-exempt status had been granted. With saviors like that, the Athenaeum is now a place of celebration. (Courtesy of Indiana Landmarks.)

When Indianapolis banker Otto Nicholas "Nick" Frenzel III got news that the foundation was tax exempt, he sent an unsolicited check for $25,000. Lou Kigin, an eccentric retired accountant, brought in $5,000. (Kigin, for unclear reasons, would never pay more for a used car than its equivalent value, by weight, in hamburger.) Kigin later donated hundreds of hours to the cause as well, as did scores of skilled volunteers. (Courtesy of Indiana Landmarks.)

One of those volunteers, Kipp Normand, discovered two long-forgotten murals written in German fraktur on the walls of the Rathskeller. The murals were whitewashed in 1918 as the Athenaeum was attempting to purge its German identity. Normand painstakingly restored them himself. Who knows what similar treasures might have been found in the Maennerchor, pictured here, had it not been towrn down. (Courtesy of Indiana Landmarks.)

Pictured here is the east face of the Soldiers' and Sailors' Monument, designed by Bruno Schmitz, a German architect. It was the first US monument dedicated to the common soldier as well as the largest outdoor memorial in the state. (Courtesy of Indiana Landmarks.)

Freezing temperatures would savage plumbing in the venerable old building, not to mention presenting an inconvenience to the Rathskeller's few remaining customers or the Turners' few remaining gymnastics students. (Courtesy of Indiana Landmarks.)

Neglected like so much of the Athenaeum, the Basile Theatre at the Historic Athenaeum offers a variety of entertainment and cultural options including live performances, speaking engagements, and film screenings. (Courtesy of Indiana Landmarks.)

Pictured here is one of the decorative touches that make the Athenaeum a visual delight. (Courtesy of the Athenaeum Foundation.)

Though this was a World War I poster, the saying applies to all those who were determined to carry on the traditions and heritage of Indianapolis. (Courtesy of Library of Congress.)

The Athenaeum Foundation successfully submitted through IUPUI a proposal to the Max Kade Foundation in New York, which provided a grant to establish the IUPUI Max Kade German-American Center in the Athenaeum. It maintains an office and seminar space in the Athenaeum to this day, shared by the Indiana German Heritage Society and the Athenaeum Turners, original owners of the building. The center's mission is to support German-American studies through research, teaching, and service. The Max Kade Center did more than keep the Athenaeum's Teutonic soul alive; it re-established a connection with IUPUI that had been severed when the School of Physical Education, originally founded as the Normal College of the North American Gymnastics Union (National Turners) vacated the building in 1970. It also furthered the Athenaeum's tax-exempt mission as an educational organization. Geist—German for spirit—had returned to the building, and the Biergarten. (Courtesy of the Library of Congress.)

While the Athenaeum Foundation was renovating the new YMCA, restoring the Rathskeller, and constructing a new roof, three of the members of the core group, Giles Hoyt and Ruth and Eberhard Reichmann, quietly labored to retain the Athenaeum's soul as a center of local German culture. (Courtesy of the Library of Congress.)

Sawyer Rank, responsible for safety and security, had an alarm system installed that tended to sound in the early morning hours and force him to wake up and go check the building. An investigation revealed that a theater employee had been relocating plants from designated spots, and a vent blowing heat against the leaves had been triggering the motion detectors. Rank also discovered flammable chemicals and other hazardous materials near the dressing rooms and tried to dispose

of them. The theater people balked, as they needed them for their sets. The foundation managed to make some improvement to fire safety but failed to bring the cabaret into total compliance. Airplanes are pictured over the Indianapolis Speedway; the city was on the move and would soon regain its ascendancy. (Courtesy of the Library of Congress.)

The Indianapolis Foundation and Ruth Lilly each contributed over $100,000, and the foundation set about raising the balance through many small contributions. Bob and Tom from the popular morning radio talk show frequently called David at his rooftop perch. Dick Wolfsie, who had a popular local morning television show on WISH-TV, climbed up before dawn and did a live show from the Athenaeum's rooftop. Small donations began to pour in. The canal is pictured before and after the rebirth. (Above, courtesy of the Library of Congress; below, courtesy of Visit Indy.)

The old canal was revitalized and the Eugene and Marilyn Glick Indiana History Center is located on the canal in downtown Indianapolis. Here, costumed interpreters greet guests. As for the Athenaeum, Jim Bradford, a local businessman, took it upon himself to upgrade the Turner's liquor permit so that the Rathskeller could legally serve alcohol to the public. Word got out, and people poured in. Bradford refused payment for his services. (Jane Simon Ammeson.)

The vibrant African American neighborhood to the canal's northwest underwent a rebirth in those years. The founding of IUPUI in 1969 and its rapid expansion thereafter soon gave the area the look and feel of an urban college campus. Sarah Breedlove, the country's first self-made female millionaire of any race, was better known as Madam C.J. Walker. (Courtesy of Madame C.J. Walker Collection, IHS.)

The neighborhood to the Canal's northwest, a vibrant African-American neighborhood, underwent a rebirth in those years. The founding of Indiana University–Purdue University Indianapolis in 1969 and its rapid expansion soon gave the area the look and feel of an urban college campus. At the time, others were saving and restoring other places throughout the city. The Madame C.J. Walker Building now houses the Madame Walker Legacy Center. Built in 1927, it was designated a National Historic Landmark in 1918. (Courtesy of Indiana Landmarks.)

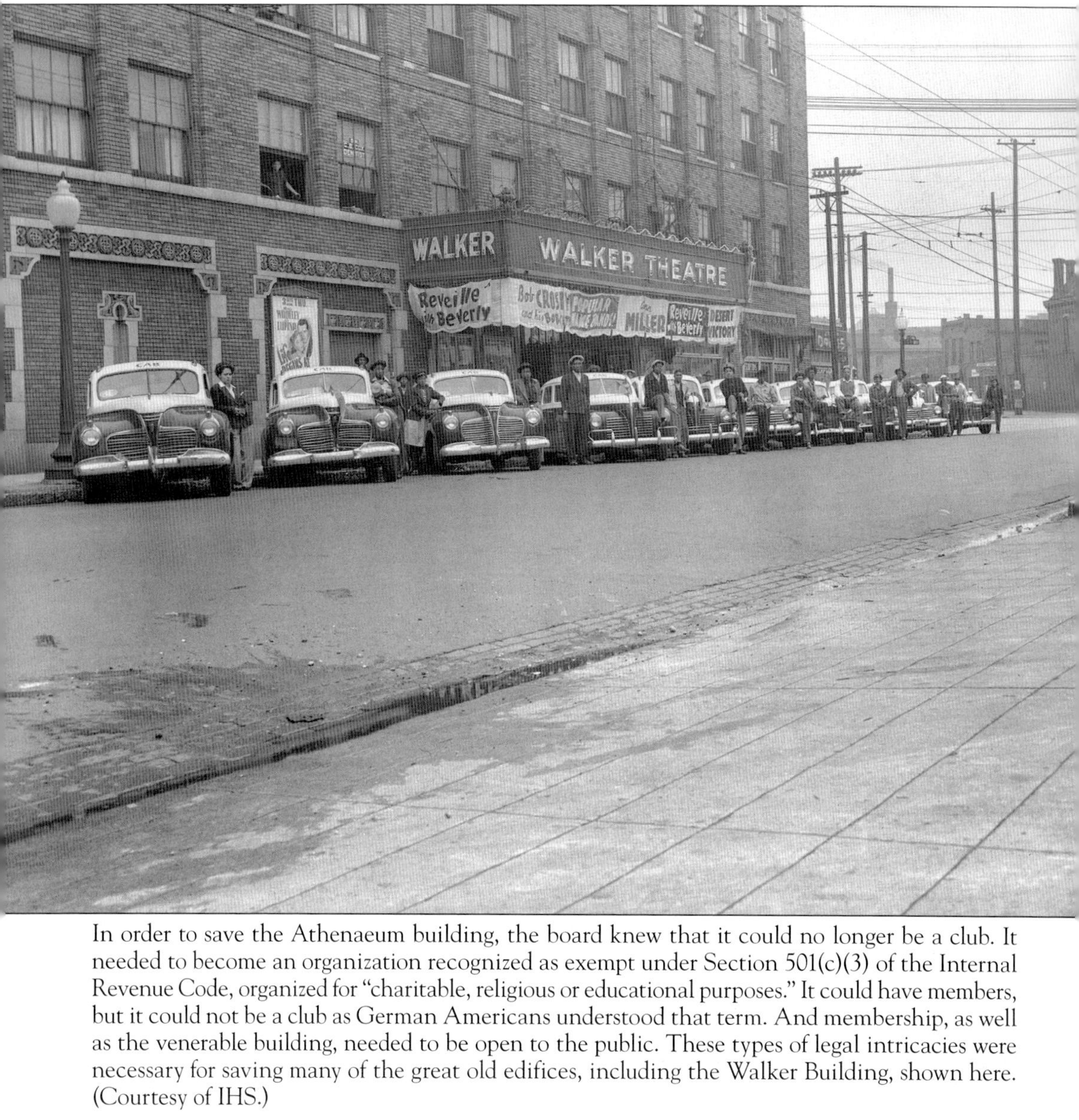

In order to save the Athenaeum building, the board knew that it could no longer be a club. It needed to become an organization recognized as exempt under Section 501(c)(3) of the Internal Revenue Code, organized for "charitable, religious or educational purposes." It could have members, but it could not be a club as German Americans understood that term. And membership, as well as the venerable building, needed to be open to the public. These types of legal intricacies were necessary for saving many of the great old edifices, including the Walker Building, shown here. (Courtesy of IHS.)

This neighborhood included the traditionally black Crispus Attucks High School, which launched the career of basketball legend Oscar Robertson, as well as the Walker Theatre, founded by Madam C.J. Walker. (Courtesy of IHS.)

Tomlinson Hall, seen in the background in this 1922 photograph, was the site for the National Prohibition Convention in 1892. It was also the site of the city market. (Courtesy of Bass Photo Co. Collection, IHS.)

Listed in the National Register of Historic Places, the Indianapolis City Market first opened in 1886 and is home to more than 25 locally owned and operated small businesses including ethnic eateries, from-scratch snacks, Tomlinson Tap 19 featuring rotating taps of Indiana craft beer, boutique goods, coffee shops, and much more. These photographs of young boys working as fruit vendors at the market in August 1908 were taken by Lewis Wickes Hine and are part of the National Child Labor Committee collection at the Library of Congress. (Both, courtesy of the Library of Congress.)

When Stutz introduced the 92-horsepower, eight-cylinder Safety Stutz in 1926 it was hugely popular, selling for $3,000 (about $41,000 today). At the time, the Ford Model T cost $300 (about $4,200 today). (Courtesy of Bass Photo Co. Collection, IHS.)

The Depression did not help sales of expensive Stutz autos. The last Stutz car was manufactured in 1934; three years later, the company had gone out of business. The Stutz headquarters are now called the Stutz Business and Arts Center, leasing space to small- and medium-sized businesses. Like the Athenaeum, it is an example of a successful restoration of an architectural treasure. (Courtesy of Bass Photo Co. Collection, IHS.)

A visitor to Das Deutsche Haus today, upon entering its grand lobby, will be greeted by the aroma of fresh latte and the sight of young people tapping on phones and laptops. A trendy coffee shop is now in the old coat-check room. At first blush, it seems to be an incongruous, even disingenuous, sight. But it is a scene that would be familiar today in Berlin, Cologne, Munich, Hamburg, and other progressive and hip German cities in old buildings that had the good fortune to survive changing times and Allied bombing during World War II . The Athenaeum has not been changed by such healthy adaptations any more than a change of clothes can alter the essence of the person who wears them. (Courtesy of Ronald Flick.)

Seven

A Community Pulls Together

One Sunday morning in 1992, a stagehand took it upon himself to cut down the century-old asbestos theater curtain, leaving it in a heap of crumpled fibers and a cloud of highly carcinogenic dust. Environmental contractor Fred Burnett was called, and in two days, his team, wearing protective suits and respirators, had removed the curtain and dust and safely and legally transported it to an EPA landfill. He also removed the pigeon guano from the attic. The Athenaeum Foundation was short of cash, so Burnett took his payment by Hofstetter adjusting his legal bill. Pictured is one of the many original stained-glass windows at the Athenaeum. (Courtesy of the Athenaeum Foundation.)

The Athenaeum Foundation gratefully renamed an east-wing room for David Willkie's efforts in raising funds for the new roof. Willkie later went on to law school and became Senator Lugar's campaign manager. As a result of these efforts, Wilhelm Bilgram was able to see the restoration project through to completion. It was a fitting final accomplishment of a kind and gentle man who was forced as a teenager to serve on the Eastern Front during the awful winter of 1944–1945. The roof was identical to the original except with more durable copper instead of galvanized steel. It will last 200 years, perhaps even longer. (Courtesy of Indiana Landmarks.)

Today, the Athenaeum straddles the past and present. Although the plants pictured here are gone, much remains the same. (Courtesy of the Library of Congress.)

The old ticket counter is now splendidly restored. (Courtesy of the Athenaeum Foundation.)

The Great Sun Council of Indiana of the Improved Order of Red Men is pictured in front of the Athenaeum in October 1908. The Athenaeum still hosts many group meetings. (Courtesy

of Bass Photo Co. Collectio, IHS.)

The Mannerchor is gone, and with it any vestige of this grand building's once-clubby nature. But the essence of the Athenaeum survives, serving the same city in the same ways more than a century after its construction. The fact that this temple to Athena stands today in much the same way as it stood in 1894 pays fitting homage to the people who created it, saved it, and continue to breathe life into it. And the building will survive and thrive and return that favor by serving generations of people yet unborn. In years to come, the gymnasium will echo to the voices and footsteps of the children of today and their progeny. (Courtesy of Indiana Landmarks.)

This sign above the bar at the Athenaeum reads, "Moderation is good and fine with me, only it itself must moderate be." The elaborate tile work is original to the building. (Both, courtesy of the Athenaeum Foundation.)

A celebration of all things Das Deutsche, the Germanfest at the Athenaeum includes Durstig games (including a beer stein relay), live wiener dog races, a strong man competition, ZwergenLand for kids, German beer and food, a bratwurst eating contest, the Octoberfast 5K, and more. All proceeds benefit the maintenance and care of the historic Athenaeum. (Both, courtesy of the Athenaeum Foundation.)

Two things conspired to change that smug picture. The first is that the Stock Association stopped keeping records and was ultimately administratively dissolved by the Indiana secretary of state for failure to file annual reports. The second is that the original stockholders began to die, and nobody kept a stock ledger or bothered to ascertain who their heirs or successors might be. By 1991, there was no Stock Association, no living stockholders, no stock ledger, and no records of who the stockholders' descendants were. Even the act under which the Stock Association had been formed had been repealed by the Indiana legislature. However, the Athenaeum Turners Club had, by some unclear means, acquired possession of a number of the old stock certificates. None of those certificates, incidentally, had even been properly endorsed over to the Turners. The celebration of German-American culture still goes on at the Athenaeum during Germanfest. (Courtesy of the Athenaeum Foundation.)

With such success, the foundation knew that its primary mission had been accomplished and the building had been saved. For his efforts, in 1992, Hofstetter received the Sandi Servaas Award for Historic Preservation from Historic Landmarks Foundation, its highest honor. On the left is J. Reid Williamson, president of Historic Landmarks. On the right is Indiana chief justice Randall T. Shepard, the Historic Landmarks Foundation chairman at that time. (Courtesy of Indiana Landmarks.)

Restoring the Athenaeum was a massive undertaking—about $1.3 million. The Lilly Endowment offered a 50 percent matching grant. A young man named David Willkie climbed onto a flat portion of the east wing roof and refused to come down until the balance was committed. Willkie was the grandson of Wendell Willkie, the 1940 Republican candidate for president. Things were turning around. The YMCA at the Athenaeum became an immediate success under the management of Dick Close, adding to the revenue stream and helping return people to the neighborhood. (Courtesy of the Athenaeum Foundation.)

But the vision of the Athenaeum Foundation would ultimately be achieved. The old coat-check room is now a trendy coffee shop, a magnet for the neighborhood and beyond. (Jane Simon Ammeson.)

Today, the Athenaeum is a lively place attracting people of all ages. (Jane Simon Ammeson.)

Indianapolis architect Ronald Flick serves on the board of the Indiana German Heritage Society, which meets at the Athenaeum. Several years ago, he was asked to recreate the original Das Deutsche Haus sign that had once topped the doorway of the building's main entrance. Ron, who is originally from Jasper, Indiana—a decidedly German city—is well known for his ability to recreate historic buildings, having designed the architecturally historic replacement of the Jasper Mill on the Patoka River in Jasper, the old train station, and the St. Joseph church balcony. He is currently involved in the renovation of the historic Astra Theatre in Jasper, which first opened in 1936 with a showing of *The Unguarded Hour* starring Loretta Young. (Courtesy of the Dubois County Visitors Center.)

Flick is a fourth-generation German American, his family having emigrated from Germany and settled in Jasper in 1848. He is a professional architect and avid historian. In addition to serving as the Strassenfest chairman in 2007 and 2008, he also served on the Strassenfest Committee for several years in the role of historian. Additionally, he has documented the pictorial history of Dubois County in his book *Jasper and Huntingburg*. (Courtesy of the Dubois County Visitors Center.)

When J. Reid Williamson Jr. died in 2017, the preservation community lost a major force, one who had a long history in the field starting in 1966, when he was hired as the first executive director of the Historic Savannah Foundation. Eight years later, he was hired to head what is now Indiana Landmarks, and he remained there for the next 31 years, turning it into one of the most effective preservation organizations in the country. Reid (right) is shown with Rick Hofstetter in front of the Athenaeum's attorney office. (Courtesy of Indiana Landmarks.)

As it has been since Das Deutsche Haus was built, the Biergarten is the place to go for fun, drinks, food, and music. (Both, courtesy the Athenaeum Foundation.)

Ron Flick, a member of the Indianapolis-based firm Pyramid Architects, has one of the largest private collections of historic Dubois County photographs and documents. In the past, he has worked as a volunteer at the Dubois County Museum and as a member of the Redevelop Old Jasper Action Coalition. By recreating the original sign, he has helped Das Deutsche Haus come full circle in many ways after overcoming adversity. (Courtesy of Ronald Flick.)

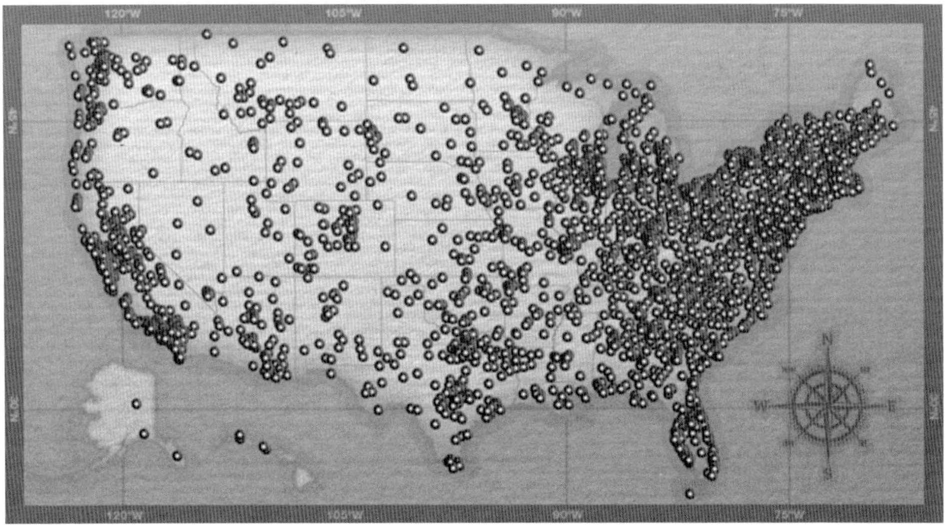